Flying to the party convention in Vancouver, the prime minister was feeling magnanimous. He turned to Joe Clark and said, "You know, I think I'll throw a fifty-dollar bill out the window and make one Canadian happy."

"I have a better idea," Clark added. "Why not toss out ten five-dollar bills and make ten people happy."

"No, no, no . . ." interrupted the ever fiscally minded Michael Wilson. "You should throw out fifty loonies and make fifty people happy."

Just then an Air Canada employee who'd recently learned he'd been laid off happened by. "Why don't you jump out yourself and make the whole country happy?"

SON
OF A
MEECH

The Best Brian Mulroney Jokes

**Edited by Mark Breslin
Researched and compiled by
Martin Waxman**

BALLANTINE BOOKS • TORONTO

Copyright © 1991 by Yuk Yuk's Publishing Inc.

All rights reserved under International and Pan-American Copyright Conventions. Published in Canada by Random House of Canada Limited, Toronto.

Canadian Cataloguing in Publication Data

Main entry under title:
Son of a meech: the best Brian Mulroney jokes

ISBN 0-345-37577-7

1. Mulroney, Brian, 1939–   — Humor.   2. Canada —
Politics and government — 1984–   — Humor.*
3. Canadian wit and humor (English).*   I. Yuk Yuk's
(Toronto, Ont.).

FC631.M85S6 1991   971.064'7'092   C91-094656-6
F1034.3.M85S6 1991

Printed in Canada

First Edition: December 1991

For Mila, with sympathy . . .

Contents

Contents

Acknowledgements

The authors would like to thank the following people: Jeff Silverman, Brian Ainsworth, Joel Axler, Noona Barlow, Don Harron, Maureen Judge, Wayne Laski, Enid Markson, Debra Morgan, Bev Nenson, Doug Pepper, Arthur Silverman, Paul Simmons, Gayle Waxman, and all the great people at Yuk-Yuk's and Random House.

Introduction

I first got the idea for this book on the morning of July 25, 1990. My producer, Brian Ainsworth, was banging at my door at the obscene hour of ten a.m. This had better be important. . . .

"Mark, quick, put on CFRB . . . They're doing an entire show on the Mulroney piece!"

The "Mulroney piece" was a short comic vignette that I had done on the CBC series, "Yuk-Yuk's: The TV Show," only a few days before. It had inspired outrage from columnists across the country. And all I had done was suggest that, when in Ottawa, visitors might like to take a "few shots" of the P.M. Naturally, I meant with a camera. It wasn't my fault that the language and iconography of photography was so close to that of assassination. . . .

I groggily tuned into the show. The host was trying to whip his audience up over this insult to the great Canadian leadership, but to no avail.

"He deserves to be shot."

". . . the worst prime minister in the nation's history . . ."

"Mulroney's a traitor and a slime and . . ."

And so on. The talk-show host finally concluded at the

end of his two-hour program that he had misjudged his audience.

But I hadn't. For the past dozen years I had whistle-stopped all across the country spreading laughs at Yuk-Yuk's comedy clubs, meeting the general—and I do mean general—public. I have never been a political comedian, never believing that the real problems of humanity had legislatible solutions. Like most of my thirtysomething generation, I was too cool, too hip, to think that politicians ever needed to be skewered. How can you debase a worthless currency? I had admired Trudeau, but the faceless bores who followed—Clark, Turner—weren't even worth the stage time.

However, this Mulroney guy was something different. The few Mulroney remarks I put into my act started getting cheers and applause, especially after the GST and free trade legislation. After each show, members of the audience would approach me with jokes about him—vicious, mean, brutal—my kind of jokes. They weren't, as my literary *sensei* Jack Kapica observed, the usual anti-government barbs, but personal ad hominem attacks on the man's most private self. These jokes had stepped over the line of good taste, and I got interested.

So I started writing them down. The collection got bigger, so I turned to Martin Waxman for help. He researched volumes of comedy material of all eras for jokes about despots and cruel or incompetent leaders. Sad to say, much of it fit. My tireless president, Jeff Silverman, and legal counsel, Wayne Laski, offered moral support and researched extradition laws. I wish I could say that my wife stood by me throughout the long, arduous task, but I am single. My cat Holly, however, did cough up fur balls on cue every time I typed the prime minister's name. All in all,

I hope you enjoy these jokes and share them with your friends.

But most of all, I hope there is no need for a sequel.

Mark Breslin
June 1991
Toronto

Fiscal Restraint

Flying to the party convention in Vancouver, the prime minister was feeling magnanimous. He turned to Joe Clark and said, "You know, I think I'll throw a fifty-dollar bill out the window and make one Canadian happy."

"I have a better idea," Clark added. "Why not toss out ten five-dollar bills and make ten people happy."

"No, no, no . . ." interrupted the ever fiscally minded Michael Wilson. "You should throw out fifty loonies and make fifty people happy."

Just then an Air Canada employee who'd recently learned he'd been laid off happened by. "Why don't you jump out yourself and make the whole country happy?"

Why does Mulroney always listen to the fiscal policies of the governor of the Bank of Canada?
Because he likes eating Crow.

Brian Mulroney was looking for a date in Times Square when he was accosted by a mugger. The mugger held a knife to the P.M.'s throat and demanded his money. Or else—he threatened—he would take his life.

Mulroney reluctantly handed over the one thousand dollars (U.S.) he had. (He never carries Canadian money.) Then he quickly grabbed seventy dollars and put it back in his money belt.

"Hey, what gives?" asked the mugger.

"GST," Mulroney replied.

Prime Minister Mulroney in a speech to the House: "I want you to know, Honourable Members, that when I took office, this country's economy was teetering on the edge of an abyss. I'm proud to say that since then we've made a valiant step forward."

While on an official visit to New York City to discuss Canada's credit rating, Prime Minister Mulroney was accosted by a street person, who asked him for a dollar.

"Do you know who I am?" an indignant Mulroney said. "I'm the prime minister of Canada."

"So find your own corner."

Mulroney grudgingly attended John Turner's first invitational charity ball and was surprised to discover he was actually enjoying himself. Dinner was a gourmet feast. And with fifty bartenders, there was never any waiting. The band played all his favourite ditties. He danced with beautiful women all night. When the party finally broke up, in the early hours of the morning, the prime minister stumbled to his car. Just as he was about to get in, he was approached by a street person begging for change.

"Get out of my way," Mulroney shouted. "I just spent the last six hours helping the likes of you. Isn't that enough?"

Thinking of ways to reduce the deficit, Mulroney, for about two minutes, considered taking a twenty-five percent cut in his pay. He discussed the idea with Mila. "It'll be tough," he said. "But if you could learn a few recipes, we might be able to fire the cook."

"And if you could learn to screw," Mila countered, "we could let go of the plumber."

The prime minister's a self-made man.

For the first time in his life, he gave a job to the lowest bidder.

Defending his policies of fiscal restraint, Mulroney was quoted as saying that inflation was the country's second biggest headache.

"That Brian," Jean Chretien remarked. "He always wants to be first."

Mulroney and Wilson were making their way along Bay Street when a homeless man asked to borrow a quarter.

Feeling the pinch of the deficit, Mulroney said to the man, "Neither a borrower nor a lender be—William Shakespeare."

"Up yours, cocksucker—Andrew Dice Clay," was the homeless man's growling response.

During question period, the Leader of the Opposition was furious.

"Mr. Prime Minister," Chretien railed on in Parliament, "you say your government practises fiscal restraint. Yet only yesterday I learned that you spent five hundred thousand dollars to have your office refurbished like Elvis's den. Now, I want an explanation—and I want de truth!"

"Which will it be?" Mulroney responded. "Will my honourable friend please make up his mind!"

Mulroney dies and goes to heaven. Just before he enters the Pearly Gates, Saint Peter asks him, "Who are you?"

"Why, I'm the last prime minister of Canada," Mulroney replies.

"And what have you done to qualify for admission?"

"You mean aside from Meech Lake and free trade and the GST and . . ."

"I mean on a personal level," Saint Peter says.

Mulroney thinks hard. "Well, in 1985, a bum accosted me for money and I gave him a nickel."

"Anything else?"

"Yes, in 1990, I passed an entire family that had been left homeless due to their shoddy economic planning, and again I gave them a nickel."

"Anything else?"

Mulroney thinks hard for another few moments before answering. "Well, no, but isn't that enough?"

Saint Peter turns to Archangel Gabriel, who has been listening to the entire exchange. "So, Gabe, what do you think we should do with this guy?"

And Gabriel replies, "Give him back his dime and tell him to go to hell!"

Canadians no longer believe in the theory of trickle-down economics.

Mulroney's trickled down on them long enough.

The Lower Chamber

The prime minister came home one day and noticed that someone had peed obscenities about him in the snow. Incensed, he called on Perrin Beatty, minister of communications, and Jean Charest, minister of the environment, and demanded that they find out who was responsible for this yellow journalism, IMMEDIATELY!

Beatty and Charest personally supervised the investigation (which included surgically removing the large chunk of snow and flying it to a lab in Sudbury). Several days later they appeared in Mulroney's office with their findings.

"Mr. Prime Minister," said Charest, "we ran over a hundred tests on the urine. And there's no question—it definitely belongs to Joe Clark."

"But," Beatty added, "the handwriting's Mila's."

Suffering from an acute case of hemorrhoids, the prime minister slinked to his doctor, who prescribed man-size suppositories. But when it was time to insert them, Mulroney was afraid he'd screw up, so he went to the parliamentary bathroom, bent over and looked through his legs in front of the mirror. All of sudden, his dick became hard and blocked his view.

"Calm down," Mulroney said to his anxious organ. "It's only me."

The prime minister was having his jaw repaired and was unable to take anything in his mouth for several weeks, so a nurse was hired to feed him rectally.

On his birthday, Mila and the nurse got together to surprise him and gave him a coffee enema.

Mulroney screamed.

"What's the matter?" Mila asked him. "Is it too hot?"

"No," the P.M. mumbled. "You know I take it black."

Mulroney's office made a terrible error and booked simultaneous appointments with the president of the United States and the pope, both of whom were visiting at the time.

"Who shall I send in first?" an aide inquired.

"The pope," Mulroney replied. "I only have to kiss his ring."

A civil servant, the owner of two lovebirds, was quite upset when he took his pets to the veterinarian. "I'm really worried about them. They haven't moved their bowels all week."

The doctor examined the birds and noticed the cage was lined with a map of Canada. "Do you always use Canada as a lining?"

"Actually," said the man, "I work in the prime minister's office and I usually use copies of his old speeches. But this week, the Polish guy with the chicken beat me to them."

"Well, that explains it," the veterinarian said. "These lovebirds are perceptive creatures. They're holding back because they know the country's taken all the crap it can."

Hoping to drum up some Arab financing, Mulroney and Wilson are travelling across the Sahara on camel. Just after noon, when the sun is hottest, the camel begins to be sluggish and Wilson figures out that the poor beast needs water. So they make their way to an oasis, but try as they might, they can't seem to make the camel drink.

Finally Wilson comes up with an idea. "Let's use the theory of trickle-down economics. I'll hold the camel's head in the water, and you suck his asshole. The water will get into his system for sure."

"Terrific concept," the prime minister says. However, after about ten minutes, he starts to gag.

"What's wrong?" Wilson asks.

"You may have his head down a bit too deep," Mulroney replies. "I'm swallowing a lot of sediment from the bottom."

What do Paul McCartney and Mila have in common?
They both blow a little dope.

Why does the prime minister have such bad breath?
Because George Bush loves baked beans.

At a medical convention in Winnipeg, a group of physicians was discussing the advanced state of medicine in their respective countries. A doctor from Great Britain bragged that if they took a heart from one man and transplanted it into another, that second man would be up and looking for work in five weeks.

"In ze fatherland," a German medic said, "if ve take an organ from any racial minority and transplant it into an Aryan, he vill not only cleanse and purify the body part, he vill be vital and looking for vork in two veeks."

"That's nothing," a Canadian doctor replied. "In Canada, we took an asshole from the Eastern Townships, transplanted him to Ottawa, and in one day half the country was looking for work."

The prime minister and Michael Wilson are travelling from Montreal to Ottawa by Via Rail, when into their compartment walks Dalton Camp. The three men discuss the gravity of the economic situation, and the whole time, Camp notices Mulroney can't stop scratching his elbow.

At one point, the prime minister dozes off, and Camp whispers to Wilson, "Tennis elbow?"

"No," Wilson replies. "Hemorrhoids."

"Are you daft? I'm not talking about hemorrhoids, I'm talking about all the P.M.'s scratching."

"So am I," says Wilson. "You know the prime minister. These days he can't tell his ass from his elbow."

19

Some people claim Mulroney is a pain in the neck. Others have a much lower opinion of him.

The pressures of leadership were getting to the P.M., and one night after dinner, he slumped in his favorite chair, drink in hand, and just stared blankly at the TV screen.

Thinking she would cheer him up, Mila walked over and started to kiss him. She started on his neck then moved down his back. . . .

"Oh, please, Mila, get off!" he barked when she reached his bottom. "Don't you know I get enough of this in caucus!"

Did you hear the new Mulroney stamp had to be recalled hours after it was issued?
People kept spitting on the wrong side.

"And how do you plan to use this artificial vagina?" the sex shop owner asked the prime minister.

"That's none of your business," Mulroney shot back.

"I'm sorry. I didn't mean to pry. It's just if it's a food item, I don't have to charge GST."

Three physicians were bragging about how easy their morning operations were.

"I operated on a German industrialist," said the first doctor. "I opened him up and he had all these gears inside. All I did was replace a defective sprocket and I was done."

"Well, I operated on a Japanese automaker," the second doctor said. "He had all these microchips inside, and all I had to do was click the old one out and the new one in."

"That's nothing," the third doctor replied. "I operated on the Canadian prime minister, and he has a sum total of two moving parts—his mouth and his asshole. And they're interchangeable."

Mulroney, Clark, and Wilson were on a trade development mission in Africa, when one of the tribal elders told them of a magical cliff. If they had the courage to shout their innermost wishes as they jumped off into the snake-infested swamp below, their innermost wishes would be granted.

Wilson went first. "Billionaire," he bellowed, and in a moment he was gliding along in the back seat of his new Rolls.

Clark was next. "Power," he cried. The next thing he knew he was CEO of Ontario Hydro.

Finally it was the prime minister's turn, but just as he was about to jump, he stubbed his toe. "Oh, shit," he yelled.

On a trade and labour junket to Mexico, Mulroney was taken to a fancy restaurant by the Mexican president. As soon as they were seated, a garnished plate of bull's testicles was brought to the president, who immediately swallowed them down.

Mulroney was envious. "Can't I get an order of those?" he whined.

The P.M. was informed that bull's balls were indeed a delicacy and that they were only able to prepare one serving a night. But at the president's insistence, the restaurant offered to make up the same special for Mulroney the following day.

Mulroney arrived and was treated to a plate of tiny testicles. He grudgingly ate them, then complained to the maître d'. "Why aren't my balls as big as *El Presidente*'s?"

"Well, Señor Prime Minister," the maître d' told him, "sometimes the bull wins."

The Chretiens are a tried-and-true Liberal family and have been for generations.

One Sunday, not too long ago, Jean Chretien was in his (former) riding to attend the christening of his newest grandson. But when the priest asked the boy's father what he was going to name the baby, the man unconsciously blurted out, "Mulroney."

Outside, Jean Chretien was livid. He ranted at his own son, calling the naming a disgrace and personal humiliation that rivalled his defeat against John Turner.

"But, Papa," said Chretien's son. "I couldn't help it. I was holding the baby in my arms, when I looked down and noticed a big grin on his face. A moment later, he was soaking me."

Not that the prime minister is crooked . . .

But last week he swallowed a nail and it came out a corkscrew.

Prime Minister Mulroney was making a speech to native leaders on the anniversary of the Oka uprising. And like all his speeches, it was short on substance but long on wind.

"I pledge a swift land-claims settlement," the P.M. said.

The crowd shouted, "Oompah, oompah!"

The P.M. paused and nodded in appreciation. "I pledge a better education system," he continued.

"Oompah, oompah!"

"I pledge more money for all native causes despite our current policy of fiscal restraint."

"Oompah, oompah, oompah!" the audience roared.

Finally Mulroney finished his oration and was given a tour of the reservation. At one point the grinning P.M., obviously pleased with himself, almost tripped. "Careful, Mr. Prime Minister," his guide warned him. "Don't step in the oompah."

The Not So Honourable Member

The prime minister was inspecting the troops just before they embarked on a tour of service in the Middle East. Everything was going well, when one of the women in the corps whispered to the P.M., "Sir, your barracks door is open."

"I beg your pardon," Mulroney said.

"Your barracks door is open."

"Arrest this woman," Mulroney commanded.

"But, sir," she pleaded. "I'm trying to tell you your fly's undone."

Mulroney felt between his legs, repaired the damage, and was a bit flustered by the snafu he almost caused.

"Tell me," he said to the woman. "When you looked into the . . . uh . . . barracks, did you notice the soldier salute?"

"Afraid not, sir. All I saw was a disabled vet, collapsed on his overstuffed duffel bags."

Prime Ministers Mulroney and Major and President Bush were on a high-level mission to the Middle East, when their plane was hijacked and taken to Iraq.

"I'm not an unreasonable man," Saddam Hussein said. "I'm willing to let you go if the sum total of your penises equals one foot."

Bush snapped out his organ—seven and one-half inches. Major was next, four inches. Finally it was Mulroney's turn. He reached inside his pants, and after a short debate, he was measured to be half an inch long. Hussein let them go.

On the plane ride back, Bush said, "If it wasn't for my seven and one-half inches, the world would be at the mercy of a madman."

Major added, "Well, without my four inch contribution the world would have been blown to kingdom come."

"I'll tell you something," Mulroney said. "The world would really be in for it, if it weren't for my hard-on."

The prime minister hurried down to his Parliament Hill pharmacist. "Give me the strongest aphrodisiac you have," he said to the gentleman behind the counter, then added, "I have a couple of young Conservatives coming over to discuss policy, if you know what I mean."

Mulroney was given the most powerful aphrodisiac on the market.

The next day he returned to the pharmacy and proudly asked the druggist if he had anything to soothe raw flesh.

The druggist nodded appreciatively. "Your penis, Mr. Prime Minister?"

"No," Mulroney replied. "My hand. The girls didn't show."

Brian Mulroney, John Crosbie, and Joe Clark were advised to spend several weeks in an impotence-self-help centre located on a secluded sheep ranch.

They weren't allowed any visitors or even any contact with the outside world. All day long they stared out the window and watched sheep. Nothing but sheep.

One day, Crosbie's hormone count was particularly high. "I know I'm getting better," he said. "You see that lamb over there. I wish she were Megan Follows."

"Maureen, forgive me, but I wish that ewe under my window was Margot Kidder," Clark continued.

"I just wish it were dark," muttered Mulroney.

Mulroney told Mila, "I'm honoured. I've been asked by the manager of the Blue Jays to toss out the first ball of the season."

"The way you've been acting lately, you might as well toss them both out."

Mulroney's dick is *so* small . . . (How small is it?)

It's so small that when Mila takes it in her mouth, she doesn't suck, she flosses.

Late one evening External Affairs Minister Barbara McDougall burst into the P.M.'s office, to find Mulroney humping a life-size poster of Madonna.

"Mr. Prime Minister!" she screamed.

"I know what you're thinking. But it's all right. I've got Audrey McLaughlin underneath."

The prime minister was attending Sunday Mass on Parliament Hill when the priest, in an attempt to rouse the political congregants from their usual stupor, asked, "Does anyone believe in ghosts?"

About half the congregation raised their hands.

"Now," the priest continued, "how many of you have actually seen a ghost?"

A quarter of the hands went down.

"And how many of you," the father's eyes were burning, "actually had sexual relations with a ghost?"

Only Brian Mulroney's hand stayed up.

"You mean to tell me, Mr. Prime Minister, that in these highly sophisticated, technocratic times you can actually state that you made love with a ghost?"

Mulroney turned beet red. "Forgive me, Father. I thought you said goat."

A young, good-looking Canadian male was despondent. He had everything going for him except for one thing. His penis was two millimeters long. One day he was lamenting his situation as he walked along a beach, when he turned over a bottle and out popped a genie.

The genie saw the sadness in the young man's eyes and offered him a single wish. The young man said that the one thing he wanted more than anything else was to have the biggest prick in the world.

"That's not a problem," the genie said. He nodded three times and then disappeared.

A moment later, the young man was face-to-face with Brian Mulroney.

The Mulroneys and the Bushes decided to go on a camping trip together in Banff. They hiked up Rundle Mountain, pitched their tents, set up a roaring fire, roasted Liberals, and when it came time to retire, Brian said, "Look, we're fast friends and we've known each other a long time. What do you say we switch partners, just for the night?"

There were no disagreements, so off went the new couples to couple in their respective tents.

Exhausted and spent after five minutes, Brian turned to his partner and said, "I'm having a great time here, George. Do you think the girls are?"

A couple of members of Mulroney's staff were in the middle of their three-hour lunch when the conversation got around to the P.M.

"You have to admire Brian Mulroney," one woman said. "No matter how many companies he's driven to bankruptcy, how low he's sunk, or how lousy he's doing in the polls, he always dresses well."

"And so quickly," the second woman added.

An elderly woman stopped at Mulroney's office and said, "I demand to have intercourse with the prime minister."

"You mean an interview, don't you?" the P.M.'s aide sheepishly asked.

"No, I mean intercourse," the woman retorted. "I want to see for myself the nuts that are running this country."

Mulroney was visiting the Canadian contingent in a remote part of Saudi Arabia and after a few days got a bit horny. "What do you do for recreation around here?" he asked the commanding officer.

"Well, Mr. Prime Minister, it's pretty slim pickings for most of the month, till the roving pack of camels makes its rounds. . . ."

"Camels? That's disgusting," the prime minister said.

But when they arrived a few days later, Mulroney was heard to mutter, "When in Rome . . ." as he began humping the first camel in sight.

At that point the C.O. came by. "Mr. Prime Minister," he said, "You're free to do whatever you like, of course. It's just most of us ride the camels to the whorehouse in the next town."

There was a period of time when Mulroney was stranded on a desert island with a female NDP fundraiser.

After a month, the fundraiser was so disgusted with what she was doing that she killed herself.

A month later, the prime minister was so disgusted with what he was doing that he buried her.

GST: Gin-Soaked Tory

Brian Mulroney often frequents taverns in Hull and challenges the bartender to Dan Quayle's favourite game. In exchange for free drinks, the prime minister allows himself to be blindfolded and then identifies whatever liquor the bartender pours—by type of alcohol *and* brand. And if at any time he fails the test, he agrees not only to pay for all the booze he's consumed, but also to buy a round for the house.

One evening he was doing especially well.

"Scotch," he roared as he downed his fifth double.

"Yes," the bartender said. "But what kind?"

Mulroney motioned for another shot. "Chivas Regal," he regally said.

The bartender grimaced and poured some more.

"Rye whiskey," the P.M. announced jovially. "Canadian Club."

Once again, the bartender was forced to go on. He handed the prime minister another glass.

"Vodka," Mulroney bellowed. "Absolut."

It was near closing time, and the bartender, no longer amused by the prime minister's antics, ducked down behind the counter and pissed into a glass.

Mulroney swished the liquid around his mouth. "If I'm not mistaken, this is urine," he said.

"Yes," the bartender replied. "But whose?"

Over dessert at 24 Sussex, Mulroney whispered to Mila, "Drinking makes you absolutely gorgeous."

"I don't drink," Mila replied.

"Yes, but I do."

Mulroney was staggering down Sparks Street when Audrey McLaughlin approached him and said, "Every time I see you on the street, you have a bottle in your hand."

The P.M. belched. "Gee, Audrey, I can't keep it in my mouth all the time."

As the keynote speaker at an interfaith religious conference, a soused Mulroney proclaimed, "I don't have to apologize for my actions to anyone. I'm a self-made man."

"Well," whispered a rabbi in the audience. "That relieves the Almighty of a tremendous burden."

Michael Wilson got a call at four o'clock in the morning to come down to police headquarters and bail out a besotted Brian Mulroney, who'd run his car into the Rideau Canal.

"Exactly what evidence do you have against the P.M.?" Wilson asked the arresting officer.

"Well, sir. When I arrived at the scene of the accident, the prime minister was in a heated argument with the minister of transport."

"And what's the matter with that?"

"The minister of transport was nowhere in sight."

In his spare time, Mulroney relaxes by composing ribald drinking songs.

But he rarely gets beyond the first few bars.

In a packed Sudbury bar that was hosting a Conservative fundraiser, a local who'd had a bit too much to drink stood up and announced, "I'd work a hundred times harder for Brian Mulroney than anyone else."

Hearing this, one of Mulroney's aides approached the man. "The prime minister appreciates your support," he said. "By the way, what do you do?"

"I'm an undertaker," was the man's reply.

Two pink elephants, five green snakes, and a yellow rhinoceros walked into a Parliament Hill tavern. "You're early," said the bartender. "The prime minister isn't here yet."

After he was first elected, Mulroney spent the night carousing in his favourite bar. "Great news, Brian," said the bartender.

"That's Mr. Prime Minister to you," Mulroney corrected.

A few more acquaintances came in. Each in turn said, "Hey, congratulations, Brian."

"That's Mr. Prime Minister," Mulroney replied.

Soon it was closing time, and Mulroney went home veritably sloshed.

"Is that you, Brian?" Mila called when she heard the door slam.

"No, it's Mr. Prime Minister," came the slurred answer.

"You'd better hurry upstairs then, John," Mila said. "Brian will be home any minute."

Brian Mulroney drinks for the economy. He's convinced the only boom there'll be is when he falls down.

The night clerk at the Park Plaza Hotel in Toronto gets a call from a rather inebriated guest—Prime Minister Mulroney—at four o'clock in the morning.

"What time does the bar open?"

"Eleven a.m., Mr. Prime Minister."

A few minutes later, Mulroney calls back with the same question.

"I already told you, Mr. Prime Minister," says the desk clerk, "eleven a.m."

A half-hour later the P.M. calls back and the desk clerk hangs up on him.

The P.M. tries once more. "What time does the bar open?" he slurringly asks.

"Look," says the irate clerk, "I don't care if you are the Prime Minister of Canada—you are not going to be allowed into the bar before eleven tomorrow morning."

"Get in?" Mulroney says. "I'm trying to get out."

The Boy from Baie Coma

The first time he heard the election results, Mulroney immediately telephoned his parents with the good news.

"Mom—I'm the prime minister of Canada. Can you believe it—I actually won?"

"Honestly?" his mother replied.

"Do we have to go into that now?"

"I hold in my hand a cheque for five hundred Canadian dollars," said the Dief to a gathering of university grads. "This cheque goes to the young person who can best demonstrate that we are of the exact same political persuasion. Any questions?"

A young man in the front row raised his hand. "Yes, you with the large chin," Dief said. "What's your politics?"

"What's yours?" Mulroney asked.

An eleven-year-old Brian Mulroney marched into a bar and said to the waitress, "Give me a double rye in a dirty glass."

She took one look at him and said, "Do you want to get me into trouble?"

"Maybe later," young Brian said. "But right now, I just want the rye."

Young Brian lusted after a three-speed bike more than anything else in the world. He asked his father if he could have one. His father said he could if Brian promised to behave for a month.

After a week of trying to be a decent human being, young Brian figured he could never make it for a month. So he went to his mother to renegotiate the agreement. His mother, however, wouldn't budge. She did suggest that maybe if he wrote a note to Jesus, he might find it less taxing to be good.

Young Brian rushed upstairs, bolted himself in his room, and began writing: "Dear Jesus, if you let me have this bike, I promise to be a kinder, gentler person for the rest of my life."

But he knew Christ would never buy that, so he ripped up the note. He tried again: "Dear Jesus, if you let me have this bike, I promise to be good for the rest of the month. . . ."

But young Brian realized even that was next to impossible. Suddenly he got an idea. He rushed into his parents' room and grabbed the statue of the Virgin Mary his mother kept on her dresser, stuffed it in a shoebox, and wrote: "Dear Jesus, if you ever want to see your mother alive again . . ."

Two mischievous twins were sent home from school with a note saying, "Dear Mrs. Jones: Your two boys claim their names are Mulroney and Wilson. Is this true or are they trying to make me look like a fool?"

Mrs. Jones responds, "Dear Teacher: The name is Miss Jones, not Mrs.; and if you had two little bastards, what would you call them?"

Mulroney's grandfather was a constant source of inspiration to his young grandson. When Brian was eight, all the boys on the block had bicycles, and so young Brian said to his grandpa, "Can I have one, too?"

His grandfather said, "Brian, does your dick touch your asshole?" Brian shook his head no, and his grandfather replied, "Then, sorry, you can't have a bike."

As a teenager, young Brian wanted a ten-speed more than anything else in the world. He begged and begged and begged his grandfather, who again asked him if his dick touched his asshole. Brian sadly said no, and his grandfather told him to forget about the ten-speed.

When he was off to college, young Brian heard that great things happened in the back seat of a car, so he went crawling to his grandfather, who said, "Brian, does your dick touch your asshole?"

A big grin appeared on Mulroney's face. "I'm a man now," young Brian answered. "Yes, it does."

"Then go fuck yourself," his grandfather replied.

Brian Mulroney was in his final year at law school when his dad, passing through town on business, decided to pay him a surprise visit. Though it was quite late, Mulroney senior made his way to his son's frat house and knocked at the door. When no one answered, he banged louder and kept it up until a sleepy voice from the second floor rasped, "What do you want?"

"Is this where Brian Mulroney lives?" his father asked.

"That's right," the voice answered. "Dump him on the back porch."

"I need to know," said the V.P. in charge of personnel for a large American subsidiary to which a young Mulroney had applied, "do you consider yourself an honest attorney?"

"Are you kidding?" Mulroney replied. "I'm so honest I paid my father back the entire twenty thousand dollars he loaned me for university after my very first case."

The V.P. was impressed. "And what case was that?"

Mulroney broke into a sweat. "The one where he sued me for the money."

A younger, gentler Brian Mulroney became engaged to Mila, and they rushed off to the doctor, a friend of his wife-to-be's family, to process their blood tests. The physician, after having a few words with Mulroney, quickly came to the conclusion that Brian had absolutely no knowledge of sexual techniques. Not only that, he was completely in the dark about anything to do with reproduction.

So, feeling he owed something to Mila's family, the doctor took Brian aside and tried to have a man-to-man chat with the future leader of Canada. Unfortunately, Mulroney was so thick-headed (but nowhere else) that nothing got through to him.

At his wit's end, the doctor finally called Mila into the examining room, asked her to remove her clothing and lie on the table, told Brian to pay close attention, and proceeded to disrobe and make love to Mila for forty-five minutes. He pulled out, sweaty and out of breath, turned to Mulroney, and said, "Now do you see what I was talking about?"

"Yes, yes," a thankful Mulroney replied. "Just one last thing, Doctor. How often do I need to bring her in?"

Before he entered politics, Mulroney had a summer job as a junior civil servant. Part of his responsibilities included touring around the countryside performing odd jobs and writing a report for the Ministry of Agriculture.

He arrived at the first farm, where the farmer didn't trust anyone who worked for the government. The farmer took Mulroney out to a barren one hundred-acre field, showed him a truckload of manure, and instructed him to spread it all over the field by dark.

Well, Mulroney worked as hard as he could and sure enough completed the task.

This impressed the farmer, who decided to go easy on Mulroney the next day. So he handed him a large sack of potatoes and told him to separate them into two piles, large and small.

But after ten hours, Mulroney was stymied. He had only managed to separate a handful of the spuds.

"I give you a simple sortin' job," the farmer told Mulroney, "and you go and botch it. Yet yesterday you outdid yerself. What gives?"

"I'm good at spreading bullshit," Mulroney answered. "But making decisions—now that's hard."

After Meech Lake fell through, Trudeau couldn't help publicly criticizing Mulroney for his stupidity and lack of leadership.

"Look, mister," Mulroney said to him one day on the street. "Why don't you leave me alone? You're old enough to be my father."

To which Trudeau replied, "That's entirely possible. What was your mother's name again?"

Many years ago, a psychiatrist was showing a visiting shrink the latest treatment techniques in his newly built super-charged asylum. They opened one door and saw an energetic young man shooting pucks at a net. When they asked him what he was doing, the young man replied that when he gets out, he's hopeful about going professional and joining the Leafs. In the next room, there was a second man, hitting baseballs. He told the doctors that when he gets out, he believes he has the potential for a terrific future as a shortstop with the Blue Jays. Finally they came to the last room, where they found a young but grizzled Brian Mulroney, jerking off into a giant bag of pecans. The psychiatrists asked what he was up to and Mulroney said, "I'm fucking nuts, man. I'm going to be the P.M."

B.M. the P.M.

A skinhead was walking by Lake Ontario when he noticed someone drowning. Without a moment's hesitation, he jumped in, swam out, and pulled the man to shore, whereupon he realized it was Brian Mulroney.

"I want to thank you for saving my life," the prime minister said. "Now if there's anything I can do for you . . ."

"There's one thing, man," the skinhead replied. "Don't tell anyone it was me."

Mulroney knew that if the Gulf War had escalated, the government would have pressed him to fly over and personally give the Canadian troops a pep talk. Preparing himself for the task, the P.M. glossed over a book about Napoleon, who apparently wore a red uniform to battle so his army wouldn't panic if he were wounded. Suitably inspired, Mulroney sent for his tailor and immediately ordered a half-dozen pairs of brown pants.

"Mr. Prime Minister," a deputy called from the next room. "Andrea Pepper of the CBC wants to know what you plan to do about the abortion bill."

"Oh, shit," Mulroney stuttered. "Um . . . tell her I'll send a cheque in the morning."

What characteristics does Brian Mulroney possess that made him lust after the leadership in the first place?

Psychologists believe it's because of his constitutional makeup: fifty percent greed, fifty percent malice, and fifty percent ego.

That adds up to 150 percent, but Mulroney could never balance his budget anyway.

What's the Canadian definition of a running gag?
Brian Mulroney.

At a dinner party at 24 Sussex, Mulroney was trying to impress the importance of frugality on the director of the National Gallery.

"You see that picture on my wall," the P.M. said. "It's an original Renoir. And I bought it for just $700. . . . It's one of the few he ever did in ballpoint."

What do you call an Irish Canadian with half a brain?
Mr. Prime Minister.

How do you make Mulroney laugh on Monday?
Tell him a joke on Friday.

Why does everyone in his constituency look up to the prime minister?
He was born poor and honest, and he worked day and night to overcome his disabilities.

Mulroney was waxing philosophic: "I believe my greatest responsibility as prime minister of this great nation is to do the greatest good for the greatest number."

"What do you mean by the greatest number?" Wendy Mesley asked him.

"Number one."

What's the only mediocre product yuppies will buy?
Brian Mulroney.

A doctor, an engineer, and Brian Mulroney were arguing about whose profession came first. The doctor claimed that since Eve was created by the removal of Adam's rib, his was the oldest profession. The engineer claimed that creating the world out of chaos was an amazing feat in engineering.

"Maybe so," said the prime minister. "But who do you think created the chaos?"

What's the difference between the prime minister and yogurt?
Yogurt has culture.

Mulroney was in the process of interviewing secretarial applicants when a sexy young woman paraded in.

"Make yourself comfortable," the prime minister purred. "I'm just going to conduct a simple test. Now, I want you to take down whatever I say. Ready? Your skirt, your bra, your panties. . . ."

Mulroney goes to the barber, who asks him when he's planning the next election. The P.M. launches into a long-winded speech about national unity and economic prosperity going hand in hand.

A few minutes later the barber asks him again. This time the P.M. expounds on the virtues of the GST and the need to reduce the deficit.

The barber asks him a third time, at which point an angry Mulroney says, "So tell me, are you a Liberal? Is that why you're so interested in the election?"

"Actually, I don't care about it at all," the barber replies. "It's just that every time I mention it, the hair on the back of your neck stands on end."

What do an atheist and Mulroney's plans for national unity have in common?
Neither has a prayer.

Where does Brian Mulroney stand on the burning issues facing Canada in the '90s?
Aside.

A poll was conducted to determine who was the most corrupt prime minister Canada ever had. To the astonishment of the public, Mulroney placed third.

He bribed the pollsters.

Mulroney called Clark into the P.M.O. to inform him he was being promoted to minister of the Commonwealth.

"But Quebec is on the verge of separation, and we have no other colonies," Clark stated.

"So what," Mulroney replied. "We have ministers of Finance and Employment."

In a recent political survey, it was estimated that fifteen percent of the Canadian public believes the prime minister is fit to govern the country.

In a related survey, it was estimated that fifteen percent of the Canadian public also believes Elvis is alive.

Why does the prime minister sound so saccharine?
Because he's always eating his words.

Why would Mulroney never be eaten by cannibals?
Because he's too hard to swallow.

Several York University psychologists decided to conduct an experiment to determine if the pets of people from certain walks of life picked up any of their owners' habits.

First they put an osteopath's dog in a room full of bones and the dog immediately set out to reconstruct them. Then they tried a serial killer's dog, who immediately began to bury them. Finally they brought in the prime minister's dog, who quickly ate all the bones, fucked the other two dogs, and then denied everything.

Why can't you circumcise Mulroney?
Because there's no end to that prick.

Brian Mulroney has the highest regard for truth. He only uses it on special occasions.

A fuming Brian Mulroney burst into the CBC National newsroom and bellowed for all to hear, "Is this the tax-sucking TV network that did the story about me being a lying, conniving opportunist?"

"I'm afraid not, " said the anchorman. "We never repeat old news."

Did you hear that the P.M.'s opening a Kentucky Fried Chicken franchise?
He's only going to serve right wings.

A Levelled Playing Field

Explaining the sorry state of the Canadian economy, Jean Chretien blamed it on the fact that the prime minister lives in a two-storey house.

"De prime minister says GST will reduce our deficit," Chretien thundered. "He also say free trade is good for de country. . . . Dose are his two stories."

If you were mountain-climbing in the Rockies and you happened to run into Brian Mulroney and Michael Wilson, who would you push off first?
Mr. Wilson. Business before pleasure.

Camping near the Nahanni, Audrey McLaughlin was shocked to see the prime minister canoeing down the river shouting at the top of his lungs, "NO! NO! NO! NO! NO!"

She spotted Mila on the other shore and, against her better judgement, said to her, "Shouldn't we do something to help your husband before he drowns?"

Mila shook her head. "Thanks all the same, Aud, but Brian's just dandy and fine."

"How can you say that?" the NDP leader inquired.

"Because all week long, he's an American yes-man. And on weekends he likes to wind down."

During a visit to the Northwest Territories, Mulroney was caught in a blustery blizzard and managed to get the last hotel room in town. George Bush happened to be caught in the same situation, and Mulroney was a bit surprised when Bush appeared at his door.

"Terrible, terrible storm this is," Bush said. "I sure would appreciate your letting me bunk in with you. Considering the gravity of the situation."

"My pleasure and my honour," Mulroney replied.

The two leaders retired to Mulroney's double bed. Later that night, Mulroney felt an erect penis against his thigh. He didn't move. Then he felt the penis inching up his body and eventually making its way to his mouth.

When he got home, he told Mila what happened.

"And what did you do?" she asked.

"What could I do? He's the president."

During one of the Big Seven Summits, Prime Minister Mulroney was feeling horny and wanted a date for the night. Three beautiful women were sent up to his room—a blonde, a redhead, and a brunette. Mulroney turned to the blonde and said, "I am the prime minister of Canada. How much do you charge for one night?" The blonde said, "A thousand dollars."

"In the old days, maybe," Mulroney said. "But right now we're on a policy of fiscal restraint."

He asked the same question of the redhead and she replied, "Five hundred dollars."

"Still too much," said the almost desperate P.M.

Finally the brunette piped in, "Mr. Prime Minister, if you can raise my dress as high as the taxes, get your honourable member as hard as times are right now, and screw me the way you're screwing the Canadian people, it won't cost you a damn thing."

Mulroney, Bush, and Mitterrand were on a train in Europe when it suddenly stopped dead in its tracks.

First Mitterrand went forward to reason with the engineer in the hopes that he could get the train rolling again. When that didn't work, Bush sent a CIA operative to assassinate the engineer and replace him with an American. And when that didn't work, Mulroney said, "Leave it to me." So he closed the blinds and said to the other two men, "Look, we're moving now."

While on an envoy to a small African country, Mulroney, Bush, and Mitterrand were found guilty of gang-banging a native woman. Since the crime was a sexual offence, the penalty imposed was also sexual. Each was sentenced to lose his penis.

However, since the country's chieftain believed in freedom of choice, the three convicted heads of state were allowed to request the way in which their punishment would be carried out.

Mitterrand, who grew up in the land of the guillotine, cried, "Chop it off."

Bush, who was a card-carrying member of the NRA, cried, "Shoot it off."

Finally it was the prime minister's turn. "Jerk it off," Mulroney said.

Mulroney was complaining of a toothache. He went to his dentist, who informed him he'd have to do a root canal. "But it's nothing serious," his dentist said. "I'm using a local anaesthetic."

The P.M. said, "You know my position on free trade and a level playing field. Use the imported stuff."

Mulroney visits his psychiatrist. "Doctor, Doctor, you've got to help me," the P.M. begs. "For the last six nights I've been plagued by a recurring nightmare. It's just horrible."

"Why don't you tell me your dream?" the shrink suggests.

"It's so painful, but, well . . . all right. I'm walking along the U.S.–Canadian border and suddenly I'm running to cross it."

"I hate to say this, Mr. Prime Minister, but many Canadians are doing the same thing."

"But you don't understand," Mulroney says. "In the dream I'm trying to get *into* Canada."

Mulroney was meeting with Michael Wilson when a call came in from President Bush. Mulroney said, "Yes, Mr. President . . . yes, Mr. President . . . of course, sir . . . why, yes, that's right . . . yes, yes, yes . . . um, no . . . yes, Mr. President . . . OK, good-bye."

"Did I hear you right, Brian—you actually said no to the president?" Wilson asked. "What did he want?"

"He wanted to know if I wasn't embarrassed having to say yes all the time."

Proposing an alternative to capital punishment, Mulroney said, "A quick, painless death is too good for those murderers. We should come up with a punishment that would really make them suffer. Like opening retail stores in Canadian border towns."

Mitterrand has an audience with God. "Tell me, *mon Dieu*," he says. "How long before the French people are truly happy?"

God says, "Fifty years."

Mitterrand weeps and leaves.

Bush has an audience with God. "Tell me, God," he says. "How long before the American people are truly happy?"

God says, "One hundred years."

Bush weeps and leaves.

Mulroney has an audience with God. "Tell me, God," he says. "How long before the Canadian people are truly happy?"

God weeps and leaves.

Brian Mulroney is the type of man with whom you could be marooned on a desert island and he could justify cannibalism on the grounds of free trade.

Joe Clark and Brian Mulroney, jetting across Canada on a unity crusade, were engrossed in the nation's map. Finally Clark pointed to Saskatoon and said, "Mr. Prime Minister, I think this is a good place to jump."

Brian Mulroney and several cabinet ministers were accosted by a drunken bum on the street. Totally disgusted by the man, Mulroney launched into a tirade about how it's indolents like him who are responsible for the deficit, for the recession, for the failure of Meech Lake. . . . He concluded by saying, "And I'm willing to bet you've never earned a dollar in your life."

"You're wrong," the bum replied. "I voted for you in the last election."

Times were tough in heaven and hell, and God and the Devil decided to stop being protectionist and to negotiate a free-trade pact. But when it came time for the deal to be signed, the Devil realized he had waived away most of his sovereignty and rights.

He called in Brian Mulroney, his chief negotiator, to berate him for his concessions. "I thought it was fine," the Devil said, "when you went and turned Canada into hell. But now you've gone and turned hell into Canada."

The Unity Issue

Mila's parents wanted their daughter and new son-in-law's honeymoon to be special. So they decided to buy a tape recorder, hide it under their bed, and give the newly wedded couple a lasting memento of their first night together.

They bribed the hotel clerk at the Ritz Carlton in Montreal and managed to get the machine in and out—then decided to listen to the tape before presenting it to the Mulroneys.

"That's happiness," they heard their daughter cooing. "That's happiness . . . that's happiness . . . that's . . ."

"Wait a minute," Mila's father said. "The battery's low." He quickly replaced it and they listened again.

This time they heard Mila giggling. "*That's* a penis?" she said.

Several weeks after she married Mulroney, Mila ran home in tears to her mother.

"It's horrible," Mila said.

"It can't be that bad," said her mother, trying to console her.

"Yes, it is. You know Brian wants to be prime minister. Well, every night before we go to bed, it's the same thing. Promises, promises, promises . . . And so far he hasn't kept one. . . ."

"What!" Mulroney bellowed at Mila. "You're sleeping with the whole cabinet?"

"I bet you didn't realize they had it in for you," Mila replied.

Why does Mila always climb on top?
Because Brian can only fuck up.

After playing a round of golf at the Rideau club, the prime minister happened to be taking a shower in the locker room when he looked over and realized he was standing next to Jesse Jackson. They started a friendly conversation, and Mulroney couldn't take his eyes off the enormity of Jesse's pecker.

"Tell me, Jesse," the P.M. said, "the secret of how you got such a giant prick."

Jesse bellowed that ever since he was a young buck, just before he goes to bed, he saunters over to the bedpost, penis in hand, and gives his member three swift whacks.

That night, Mulroney decided to experiment with Jackson's routine. And just before crawling into bed, he took out his member and gave it three swift whacks against the bedpost.

Mila, who was half asleep, turned and said, "Jesse, is that you?"

How do Brian and Mila perform oral sex?
They sit at opposite ends of the bed and yell, "Fuck you."

Discovering Mila in bed with a plumber, Mulroney cried out in amazement, "My lord, Mila, what are you doing?"

Mila turned to the plumber. "Didn't I tell you he was dumb?"

On their honeymoon, Brian and Mila were under the covers; a satisfied grin was on Mulroney's face.

"Tell me," he murmured to Mila. "Am I the first man you ever made love to?"

"It's possible," Mila replied. "Your dick looks really familiar."

The prime minister's wife fell ill with a particularly severe virus and thought she was dying. "Brian," she said weakly, "the way I feel now, I may not be around tomorrow. So I have one last request."

"Anything," the P.M. replied, "short of calling a plumber."

"Well," she said coyly. "The dozen times we made love it was always in the missionary position, and I was wondering if just once—we could have anal sex."

"That's not an unreasonable request," Mulroney told her. And he proceeded to mount his wife from behind. After the ordeal was over, the two fell into a deep sleep.

Expecting to find himself a widower, Mulroney was surprised to hear his wife up and singing the next morning. She had even prepared the P.M. a huge breakfast and was in a terrific mood.

"It's a miracle. I'm completely cured," she said.

He burst into tears.

"What's wrong?" she asked. "Aren't you happy I'm still around?"

"Of course I am," he said. "It's just this has been such an emotional moment for me. Not only has your life been spared, but now I know how to save the country, too."

Mulroney dissolved Parliament early one day only to come home to find Mila sweating and panting in bed.

"Are you all right?" he asked her.

"I . . . don't know," Mila replied. "Maybe I'm . . . having a heart attack."

"Oh, my God," Mulroney said, and rushed out to call an ambulance.

Just then one of his kids screamed, "Daddy, there's a naked man in the closet."

Mulroney ran downstairs and came face-to-face with the plumber.

"For Chrissakes," he said. "Mila's upstairs having a heart attack and you're skulking around scaring the kids."

One evening after dinner, Mila and Brian were talking. "This is completely hypothetical, but what would you say," Mila asked him, "if I told you I was having a mad, passionate love affair with your best friend?"

The P.M. laughed. "You know I don't have any friends," he replied.

After several years of marriage, Mila just couldn't arouse Brian anymore (or at least make him feel the way he felt in caucus). She tried everything from sexy negligees to water sports, but still the P.M. spurned her advances.

One day, however, she was thrilled when Mulroney announced that he was going to a hypnotist to seek help for their problem. And sure enough after two visits they were back to making love the way they used to—once whenever Parliament was in session. The only problem was, during the height of passion, Mulroney would rush to the bathroom for a few minutes, then sheepishly return.

At first this didn't bother Mila, but then her curiosity got the better of her. So she followed Brian into the bathroom and saw a glazed prime minister staring at the mirror, murmuring, ''She's not my wife . . . she's not my wife . . . she's not my wife. . . .''

What does Mila do when she needs her pipes cleaned?
She calls a plumber.

Mila was awakened one night by a noise at 24 Sussex. "Brian," she said, "there's a thief in the house."

"Impossible," Mulroney snored. "I appointed them all to the senate."

Mulroney came home late one evening to find Mila crying in bed. "I wish I was fifty votes," she sobbed.

"Fifty votes," said the P.M., "Why?"

"Because then," Mila replied, "I'd be sure you loved me."

The P.M. came home after a hard day's work to find Mila stark naked in front of a mirror, fawning over her breasts.

"What's going on?" Mulroney asked.

"Oh, nothing," she said. "Except I went to the doctor this afternoon and he told me I have the body of an eighteen-year-old."

"Oh, really," he remarked, "what did he have to say about your big old ass?"

"I don't know," she told him. "He didn't mention your name at all."

The Fool on the Hill

When the P.M. kept losing his place during "Second Readings," he decided he'd better see an optometrist. The doctor sat him in front of an eye chart and instructed Mulroney to place his hand over one eye and keep the other one open, but these instructions were just a little complex for Brain to follow.

Nearing the point of exasperation, the doctor cut a hole in a brown paper bag and placed it over the P.M.'s head. "Does that make it any better?" the optometrist asked.

"I think so," Mulroney replied. "But I was hoping for something a bit more stylish, like bifocals or wire rims."

Looking to bolster his stodgy image, the P.M. spent a night at a rock club. And not wanting to be perceived as a square, he even snorted Sweet and Low.

He thought it was Diet Coke.

Getting his summer home at Meech Lake ready for a gathering of first ministers, the P.M. drove into town and purchased a box of mothballs. The next afternoon he came back and bought two dozen more.

"But Mr. Prime Minister," the crusty owner said, "you just bought some yesterday."

"I realize that," the P.M. replied. "But those goddamn moths are so speedy, they're impossible to hit."

Mulroney searches the streets of Ottawa and finally finds a tiny, obscure barber shop.

"Do you know who I am?" he asks the barber.

"No," the barber replies.

"Good. Then you can shave me."

Mulroney was surprised when he received a call from Barbara Frum to appear on "The Journal."

"Will a five hundred dollar honorarium be acceptable?" she asked him.

"Certainly," the P.M. said. "I'll give you a cheque."

Clark to Wilson: "What should we give the prime minister for his birthday? A book, perhaps?"

"I don't think so," said Mulroney, who just happened to be passing by. "I already have one."

A black-tie reception was being held in Washington. Unfortunately, Mulroney lost his invitation. He sheepishly approached the front gate and tried to gain entry.

"I'm sorry," said the doorman. "This is an exclusive event. How do I even know you're who you say you are?"

"But I'm the prime minister of Canada," Mulroney lamented.

"Listen," the doorman continued, "Mikhail Baryshnikov also arrived without his invitation, but when I asked him to prove who he was, he executed a perfect pas de deux, so I let him in. Then Jay McInerney arrived, also without his invitation, but I handed him a pen and some coke and he wrote a sharp two paragraphs on the vibes he felt that evening and how the drugs helped alleviate his sense of alienation, so I also let him in."

"Who are Mike Baryshnikov and Joe McInerney?" a puzzled Mulroney asked.

"That's it, let him in. He's definitely the prime minister of Canada."

"I'll tell you, Brian," Reagan said to Mulroney during the first round of free trade negotiations. "We need to satisfy our farmers, too. In any given year, do you have any idea how many tons of wheat the U.S. exports?"

Mulroney was eager to impress. "In fourteen ninety-two," he said, "none."

Mulroney gave a two-hour speech in Germany outlining his proposed economic recovery platform in the next election, leaving no fiscal detail unmentioned, no restraintive policy unturned. When he was finally done, he turned to the fidgety audience. "Are there any questions?" he asked.

"Just one," said the German chancellor. "Who else is running?"

A high-ranking Canadian civil servant spent his holidays scuba diving in shark-infested waters off the Florida coast.

When he returned home, he regaled his coworkers with tales of his adventures, and they were astounded that the sharks kept circling around him but left him alone.

"How did you manage it?" they all wanted to know.

"Simple," said the man. "The whole time I was there, I wore a T-shirt saying, BRIAN MULRONEY IS THE BEST PRIME MINISTER CANADA HAS EVER HAD. Not even a shark would swallow that."

A man and a woman were on the make at an Ottawa civil service soiree. "Did you hear the latest Mulroney joke?" asked the woman.

"Absolutely not," replied the man, indignantly. "And I'll have you know, I'm a personal friend of the prime minister."

"In that case," the woman said, "I'll tell the joke very slowly."

Mila accompanied the prime minister on a tour of southeast Asia. When they got home, her daughter asked her what she did.

"Well," Mila considered. "I saw a few pagodas. I spent an afternoon in a couple of rice paddies. And I ate nine thousand, four hundred fifty-six snow peas."

"Stop joking, Mom," her daughter said. "How can you be sure about the exact number?"

"You know I always keep myself busy when your father is speaking."

On a governmental junket to China, Mulroney is given a beautiful piece of silk. He takes it to a tailor in his home riding of Baie Comeau to have it made into a suit.

"*Je regrette*, monsieur," the tailor tells him. "You only have enough cloth for a jacket."

Mulroney doesn't believe him and takes it to several other tailors in town, who all say the same thing.

He carries the cloth with him everywhere. Finally he takes it to a tailor in Winnipeg who whips up a suit in three days. Mulroney can't believe it. He explains how no one could make the suit in Baie Comeau and wonders how the Winnipegger managed it.

"Simple," says the tailor. "You're not such a big man here."

Mulroney had just finished explaining his policies to a gathering of citizens in Saskatoon when one person in the crowd stood up and announced that the speech was completely incoherent and how it was insane that an incompetent like Mulroney could be running the country.

Embarrassed, the chair of the evening put his arm around the prime minister and said, "Pay no attention to that man. He just goes around repeating what he hears everyone else say."

Responding to a recent poll, where he learned he was being tolerated by as little as fifteen percent of the Canadian public, the prime minister was heard to remark, "Great, that means we're halfway there. . . ."

What's the difference between Howdy Doody and Prime Minister Mulroney?
You can't see Mulroney's strings.

What's the difference between Mulroney and a dodo bird?
One's extinct. The other ought to be.

Mulroney picked up an attractive woman in the Watergate Hotel in Washington. After a few drinks, he told her who he was and she seemed visibly impressed. "Would you like to hug me?" she said.

"You bet," the P.M. replied.

"Would you like to kiss me?"

"I sure would."

"OK, hang on to your hat, because here comes the five hundred dollar question."

The prime minister was campaigning in Edmonton when he received an urgent call from his chief of staff. "You've got to get back to Ottawa right away, sir. You can't imagine the lies they're spreading about you."

"Impossible," replied Mulroney.

"But, sir, the lies."

"They'll have to wait. I have a bigger concern in Edmonton. Here they're spreading the truth."

On a recent trip to Washington, Mulroney checked into his hotel to find two buxom blondes waiting for him in his bed.

"Don't you know who I am?" he bellowed. "I'm the prime minister of Canada, the most wholesome nation on earth. I'm a family man and a devoted member of my church. I'm no Massachusetts senator. I can't afford a scandal of this nature. . . . One of you will have to go."

Pierre Elliot Trudeau proved that a man could not be stopped from becoming prime minister simply because he was an intellectual genius.

Mulroney went even further.

He proved that a man could not be stopped from becoming prime minister simply because he was Brian Mulroney.

Wendy Mesley was trying to get an exclusive interview with Brian Mulroney after the disastrous failure of Meech Lake.

"I have nothing to say," the prime minister told her.

"I know that," Mesley replied. "Now can we get on with the interview, please."

Brian Mulroney returned to his hotel in New Delhi after meeting with the prime minister of India and requested that Mila paint a black dot on the centre of his forehead before they went to the gala dinner the Indian P.M. was hosting for them that evening.

"I don't want to insult him again," Mulroney declared. "This afternoon after I finished my progressive taxation discussions with the Indian P.M., he turned to one of his advisors, tapped his forehead, and whispered, 'Nothing there.' "

Sometime in the next century, a Canadian feels the need for a brain transplant. He goes to the doctor's showroom and inspects the current models. The brain of a sixty-year-old mathematical genius is going for five hundred dollars because of its somewhat worn condition. The brain of a twenty-five-year-old skinhead is going for one thousand dollars. And off in the corner for one hundred thousand dollars is the brain of the late prime minister Brian Mulroney.

The man asks why that brain is so expensive.

"Because," the doctor says, "it's hardly been used."

What's the difference between Socrates and the prime minister?

Socrates knew he knew nothing.

Why doesn't the P.M. play hide-and-seek?

Because he knows no one's going to go and look for him.

Things were looking bad for the prime minister. Meech Lake was a disaster. The economy was in terrible shape. Quebec and the West were threatening to separate.

So it wasn't surprising that one night he found himself on the roof of the Chateau Laurier, contemplating whether or not to jump. Just before he made the move to end his misery, an ugly old witch approached him and asked what the matter was. When he told her, she said that since she was indeed a witch, it would be her pleasure to solve the P.M.'s problems.

She waved her arms. "All right, Meech Lake is signed." She waved her arms again. "The economy is healthy, Quebec and the other provinces are getting along, and I've even thrown in a bit of deficit reduction on the side."

Mulroney was flabbergasted, but he felt the weight had been taken off his shoulders. "Thank you," he said. "Now if there's anything I can do for you."

"As a matter of fact," the witch said, "there is. I'd like you to spend the night making love to me."

Although the idea made him sick, Mulroney agreed.

In the morning, as the prime minister was lying next to the witch in her bed, she turned to him and asked, "How old are you?"

"Let's just say I'm circling fifty," Mulroney replied. "Why?"

"Don't you think that's a bit old to believe in witches?"

On a weekend retreat in Kennebunkport with President Bush, Mulroney and the president were in Bush's boat, fishing. Bush decided he had to take a leak, so he undid his pants and started peeing over the side of the deck. Suddenly a giant shark jumped up and bit Bush on the dick. Without flinching, Bush jabbed the shark in his eyes. The shark let out a yell and jumped back in the ocean, sobbing. Bush then turned to the prime minister and said, "Can you do that?"

"Of course," Mulroney replied, "if you promise you won't poke my eyes out."

What's nine inches long and hangs between Bush's legs? *Mulroney's necktie.*

Son of a Meech

John Turner arrived in hell and was being shown his damnable accommodations when he happened to pass a sewer in which Brian Mulroney was making love to Kim Basinger.

More indignant than he was over free trade, Turner turned to the devil escorting him and whined, "Mr. Vanderzalm, this isn't fair. I've been condemned to hot lava, while my honourable opponent gets to spend eternity screwing Kim Basinger."

Vanderzalm laughed. "And who are *you* to criticize Kim Basinger's punishment?"

After a particularly humiliating meeting with President Bush, the prime minister went to a Washington bar to drown his sorrows and didn't realize he was seated next to former press secretary James Brady. The two men got to commiserating, and after a few minutes Brady fell off the bar stool.

Figuring there was no way this guy could make it home on his own, Mulroney grabbed the man's wallet and found his address. Since he only lived a few blocks away, Mulroney figured they could walk it. He slipped an arm around Brady's shoulder and they started for the door. But after a few steps, Brady's legs crumpled and he collapsed to the floor. Mulroney sneered and helped him up, but a couple of feet later, the same thing happened.

Brady attempted to mumble something to the prime minister, but he was in no mood to listen. "You stinking lush," Mulroney said to him. "I have a good mind to leave you in the street. But, nice guy that I am, I suppose I'll carry you the rest of the way."

He hoisted Brady on his shoulder and dumped him on the porch of a renovated brownstone. At that point a woman came to the door.

"Madam," said Mulroney. "If I were you, I'd have a talk with your husband about his drinking."

"I will," Mrs. Brady promised, then glanced around the street. "But tell me, where's Jim's wheelchair?"

Why is the prime minister having so much trouble getting a new round of constitutional talks going?
Because no one will listen to the son of a Meech.

Did you notice how the unemployment rate's started to dip?
Mulroney's including blow jobs.

Mulroney was having dinner with Preston Manning of the Reform party when he brought out a bottle of his finest port. Manning, a teetotaler, was incensed.

"This is the ultimate insult," Manning stormed. "Why, I'd rather commit adultery than drink a single glass of port."

"Who wouldn't," Mulroney replied.

Mulroney marched into the parliamentary library and straight to the desk of one of the librarians, an uptight, lemon-sucking civil servant, and said, "Madam, I know you don't make a lot of money, and I have a proposition for you. I know the odds are against me, but I'm willing to bet five thousand dollars that by this time tomorrow, your nipples will be gone."

The librarian was completely insulted but also somewhat turned on. "All right," she agreed. And the P.M. signed a bill stating his position.

For the rest of the afternoon, the librarian was extra careful. She made sure she kept away from any sharp objects. She didn't even go home; she just sat at her desk and stayed awake all night lest some weird disaster befall her.

In the morning, she was exhausted and dishevelled, but satisfied. She was certain she had won. Shortly after the library opened, Mulroney came in, escorted by Jean Chretien. Mulroney grinned at the librarian. "Well?" he said.

With a proud expression, the librarian ripped open her blouse, yanked down her bra, and exposed her nipples. Whereupon Jean Chretien passed out. Mulroney handed the librarian five thousand dollars, reached in Chretien's breast pocket, and removed a thick stack of bills.

"What's wrong with the honourable Leader of the Opposition?" the librarian asked.

"Nothing," Mulroney replied. "I just bet him fifty thousand dollars that I could walk in here and have you show me your tits."

Mulroney was meeting with the first ministers at Meech Lake when he swam out a bit too far and began to drown. Wilson and a group of premiers sped out in the power boat to save him. They extended their hands and waved them in front of the drowning Mulroney. "Here, Mr. Prime Minister. Give me your hand," each was heard to say.

The P.M. continued to thrash.

Finally Wilson put out his hand. "Mr. Prime Minister, take my hand," he said, "take my hand." Whereupon Mulroney reached up, grabbed Wilson's hand, and was pulled to safety.

Later in the evening, the first ministers gathered around Wilson to find out the reason for his success.

"You see," said Wilson, "I happen to know Brian Mulroney very well. All of you wanted him to give. And he's a man who only knows how to take."

"This is purely hypothetical," Mulroney said to his favourite mistress. "But what would happen if you found yourself pregnant and alone?"

"That's horrible," said his mistress, practically in tears. "I'd be so hysterical, I'd probably kill myself."

"Good thinking," Mulroney replied.

"Then again," she added, "not that I'd have a choice."

On a unity mission in Vancouver, Mulroney and a few cabinet members decided to take the ferry to the island. However, the boat collided with a rock and started to go down.

"Man the lifeboats," Clark shouted. "Women and children first."

"Fuck the women and children!" Crosbie barked.

A glint appeared in the prime minister's eye. "Is there time?"

"Stop! It hurts!" Mila screamed when Brian mounted her from behind.

"You're crazy," the P.M. replied. "It feels great."

What's the difference between Rock Hudson and Brian Mulroney?
Brian's aides haven't killed him yet.

A stranger passing through Alberta stopped at a roadside bar, had a few drinks, and bellowed in a loud, drunken voice, "The prime minister is a horse's ass." When no one responded, he said it a little louder.

Finally a big, strapping cowboy came up to him and said, "Mister, those are fighting words around here."

"I'm sorry," the man said. "I didn't know this was Mulroney country."

"It isn't," the Albertan told him. "It's horse country."

Brian Mulroney and a dead skunk are lying in the middle of the Trans Canada Highway. How can you tell the difference between them?
There are skidmarks around the skunk.

A young boy from Winnipeg wrote the following letter to God:

"Dear God,
My parents are divorced and there's nothing I want more in the world than to give my mother a special gift for her birthday. But I have no money. Could you please send me one hundred dollars as soon as you can."

The child addressed the envelope simply "God," put it in a mailbox, and someone in the postal bureaucracy with a sense of the absurd forwarded the letter to the prime minister's office. One of Mulroney's aides saw it, requisitioned a cheque for five dollars, and sent it along with a signed photo of the P.M. to the boy.

A few days later, the boy sent God another note.

"Dear God,
Thanks for sending the one hundred dollars. But why did you send it through Ottawa? As usual, that bastard Mulroney clipped ninety-five percent for taxes."

Michael Wilson was strolling along the Plains of Abraham, past the statue of General Wolfe, when he heard a voice. "Bring me a horse . . ." it said.

He looked around, couldn't see anyone, and continued on his way. The next day, he went back and again heard the voice. "Bring me a horse . . ." it said.

Now Wilson was really intrigued. He told the prime minister about the incident and finally convinced him to accompany Wilson to the Plains of Abraham the following afternoon.

Suddenly, the eerie voice broke in. "I asked you for a horse and you brought me an ass."

The night before debating John Turner, Mulroney was practising his opening remarks when he felt a tug at his pant legs and heard a squeaky voice. "Glide over your words like a CBC announcer," it said. Mulroney looked down and saw the voice was coming from a frog. "Trust me," the frog said. Mulroney thought, what could he lose, and took the frog's advice.

His performance at the debate was a huge success. And throughout the campaign, the frog was constantly at Mulroney's side, whispering strategy and ideas. Mulroney always listened. And sure enough, thanks to the frog, Mulroney became prime minister of Canada.

When the campaign was over, he took the frog to Atlantic City to celebrate. Mulroney booked them into an opulent suite and personally made a special bed of mulch for the frog. But the frog begged to sleep in the same bed as Mulroney, who couldn't help but comply. "Kiss me," the frog said. What could he do? Mulroney closed his eyes, kissed the frog, and just as he did, it turned into the most beautiful fifteen-year-old girl he ever saw.

"And that, my fellow Canadians," Mulroney confessed on national television, "is exactly the way it happened, so help me God."

Jean Chretien was campaigning in a small town in western Canada. He came to a secondhand store, wandered inside, and was at once drawn to a brass sculpture of a rat. He asked the store owner how much it cost.

The retailer replied that it was at least five hundred years old and that he'd sold it twice during the last week, but both times the customers returned it, so he'd let Chretien have the rat-art for fifty dollars.

Chretien paid him and continued on his way. But suddenly he felt he was being tailed. He turned and noticed that a dozen rats were following him, and their ranks were swelling. Pretty soon a jittery Chretien was being pursued by thousands of rats.

Not knowing what to do, he passed the Saskatchewan River and threw the sculpture in. To his amazement and relief, all the rats plunged to their watery deaths.

The next day Chretien reappeared in the secondhand store.

"You're not going to try to return that rat sculpture," the owner inquired.

"Of course not," Chretien replied. "I'm here to see if you might have a brass bust of the P.M.?"

Mulroney claimed that all his life he's wanted to be prime minister in the worst possible way.

And he's succeeded beyond his wildest dreams.

About the Author

Mark Breslin, the founder of Yuk Yuk's, has an impressive string of credits in directing, and producing, and promotion of Toronto comedy, theater, and music.

Mark has been the Director of Theatre and Music at Harbourfront, hosted OECA's "The Comedy Shoppe," hosted his own two-hour radio talk show on Q107, produced "The Late Show" for the Fox Television Network, and acted as Comedy Producer for the "Joan Rivers Show." In 1990, Yuk Yuk's expanded into the television market with the debut of "Yuk Yuk's—The TV Show" on CBC.